The Key to the Gate

Principles and techniques to get past

gatekeepers to the decision maker.

A must have for anyone in

business-to-business sales.

The KEY to the GATE

PRINCIPLES AND TECHNIQUES TO GET PAST GATEKEEPERS TO THE DECISION MAKER

EKSAYN AARON ANDERSON

The Key to the Gate

Principles and techniques to get past gatekeepers to the decision maker.

A must have for anyone in business-to-business sales.

ISBN-13: 978-0990395201

ISBN-10: 0990395200

LCCN: 2014908761

Eks Communications, LLC

Saratoga Springs, Utah

This book includes accounts of real-life events that have been purposed for education. As such, names, details and exact dialogue have been adjusted to suit these purposes and to provide anonymity the participants in these events. This book is designed to provide information regarding the subject matter covered. It is sold with the understanding that the publisher and author are not engaged in rendering professional legal, medical, accounting, tax, real estate or other services. If legal advice or other expert assistance is required, such advice should be sought from the appropriate competent professional(s).

Cover design:

Myntillae Nash/ Myntifresh Designs

Cover graphic artwork © 2022:

https://stock.adobe.com/images/real-estate-buy-home-honcept-gold-key-on-a-blue-background-web-banner-with-copy-space/303606366

Interior design and interior graphics © 2014:

Cindy C Bennett

Interior graphic artwork © 2014:

Depositphotos.com/Iqoncept/26152417 * Depositphotos.com/Natashin/42111753 * Depositphotos.com/Stiven/6127875

Acknowledgements

I feel deeply grateful

—to my wife and companion, Katie, for her assistance in editing, her insight, patience, encouragement, and suggestions.

—to my brother, Leland, for his thoughtful suggestions.

—to my parents, EksAyn and Patricia, for teaching me a good work ethic and the value of education.

—to Kevin for believing in me.

—to Jason Webb for his help in getting this book ready for print.

—to Brady Bastian for his friendship and feedback.

—to Cindy C. Bennett and Myntillae Nash for their contributing talents.

And finally, I am grateful for the happy memory of my mother, Linda, for believing in me, helping me create my first book when I was very young, and for wanting me to draw trees the way I see them.

Contents

Foreword

Business-to-business sales are in a different league from person-to-person sales. They have their own set of rules and require a unique approach. Just as the sale is different, even getting to the point where you have the chance to share your presentation requires a unique set of skills and know-how. Anyone presenting a product, idea, or service can *approach* an organization; not everyone can get in.

Salespeople at all levels have most likely been frustrated or shut out by the obstacles present in business-to-business sales, perhaps discouraged by their inability to get access to the right people. They get "screened out" or rejected by assistants, secretaries, or other "gatekeepers" before they even have a chance to present to the decision maker. This wall stops them dead in their tracks, barring a potentially valuable relationship.

Even seasoned salespeople are often intimidated when selling to businesses because of fear of rejection, fear of getting the runaround when calling a business, fear of the complexity of the organization, and doubt about whether they are talking to the right people.

The experience of selling to a business isn't limited to salespeople. At some point, many people find the need to approach an organization, whether it is selling a product, idea, or service; for fundraising needs; or even just selling their personal credentials in an interview or audition. Many of these "sales" approaches are to organizations where success comes through connecting with, impressing, and convincing key decision makers.

When these key decision makers are heavily guarded by savvy gatekeepers, it can seem impossible to connect with anyone of influence. However, I'm going to show you that influence isn't always where you expect, and there are specific principles and techniques that can work wonders in getting you to where you want to be.

Principles vs. Techniques

Many sales books are filled with techniques and scripts, supposedly telling you exactly how to approach almost every situation. This book is different. Though *The Key to the Gate* offers some key techniques for getting appointments, it focuses heavily on the principles that underlie the techniques. To really understand this, a distinction needs to be made between principles and techniques.

The world works on principles. These principles work whether you think they do or not. Principles are timeless and real. They don't just work once. They don't change—they work across many situations and over time.

As an example, gravity is a true principle. You can learn to profit from gravity by understanding it or you can ignore it to your peril. Many have learned to profit from the principle of gravity. Owners of hydroelectric dams, skydiving companies, and ski resorts are all examples of organizations that understand, respect, and have profited from the principle of gravity. In contrast, many a careless hiker or climber has been injured or killed by not fully respecting or, at the very least, being careless toward the principle of gravity. Whether you believe in gravity or not, gravity itself does not change.

Another example of a principle is honesty. Honesty, even when it is difficult to be honest, breeds trust—trust for yourself and for others as well as an ability to trust other trustworthy people. When you try to short circuit the principle of honesty, you either quickly or eventually lose the trust of others and many times end up not even trusting yourself.

Principles are truths that work across virtually all situations. Techniques, on the other hand, are the "how-to's" that may or may not work in every situation. For example, the principle that crops need water to grow is evident and applies to nearly all crops. However, the techniques I use to water my crops can vary. My techniques may include using a sprinkling system or an irrigation ditch. I can even water my crops by throwing water balloons at them. The principle that I must water my crops remains constant even if my techniques vary.

It is important to learn both sales principles and sales techniques. However, if I had to choose between the two, I would choose principles. By fully understanding just one sales principle, I may be able to create 50 different appropriate sales techniques. On the other hand, if I rely solely upon my use of one technique, it probably will not work in every situation. More importantly, I may know the technique, but if I lack understanding of the principle behind it, I could apply the technique at the wrong time or in the wrong way.

This book attempts to assist in what is a relatively short-term process: the process of getting appointments with key decision makers. Because this process is short, some salespeople may be tempted to think that they can use less-than-honest techniques and ignore the principles of honesty and integrity in their quest to get appointments. Though it is possible that a dishonest technique may "work" in the short run, dishonesty in any form is a recipe for failure, wasted time, and broken sales relationships.

Good salesmanship is the art of building trust and influence. This trust and influence can only last if built upon true principles. In building your sales network, you must build on true principles or your business will likely be short lived and non-fulfilling. If you want to build a lasting sales, business, or personal foundation, you must build it on true principles of honesty, integrity, hard work, and other timeless principles.

It will take work to apply the principles in this book. They are not short cuts, but can be used by people who are looking to learn from my experience and willing to invest the time needed to develop the skill. I have been involved in sales for a long time. I have successfully sold at various levels—from door to door sales, to selling to large organizations. I have learned valuable sales principles and hope that you will learn from my experience and at the same time combine the principles in this book with your own talents, personality, and twist.

The Gate and the Key

Decision makers are bombarded daily with salespeople pitching their product or service. If every CEO talked to every salesperson that wanted time with them, they would never get anything else done. So "gates" rise up to keep salespeople out. These gates may include the decision maker's over-packed schedule or the fact that he doesn't want to be bothered by someone trying to sell to him. Anything blocking access to the decision maker could be considered a gate. Somehow you have to find your way through the gate. Most of the time, you have to get past the gatekeeper to get there. Secretaries and receptionists act as gatekeepers. It is their job to keep those barriers in place and filter who is worthy of the decision maker's time.

The gatekeeper has the key to get you through the gate and in front of the decision maker. What you do once you get the appointment is for another book.

First you need the gatekeeper to get you 30 minutes in front of the decision maker so you have a shot!

Your goal is to positively differentiate yourself to the decision maker or someone close to him—the gatekeeper. While the gatekeeper holds the key to the gate and then beyond to the decision maker, you have the ability to influence the gatekeeper. You need to leave a positive, memorable impression that lets you stand out from all the other salespeople that contact him each day. The distinguishing factors come when you act with solid principles: treat everyone with respect and as a friend, act with integrity, and be genuine and gracious. By following the principles and techniques discussed in this book, you will have gatekeepers opening gates for you.

Chapter One

Where Do I Start?

We are not interested," she said curtly and hung up the phone, cutting me off mid-sentence. Surprised by her apparent lack of manners, I sat frozen, staring blankly at the woven pattern on the cubicle wall in front of me, still stinging from her abrupt rudeness.

This wasn't the first time this had happened to me. I was tempted at this point to give up on trying to get an appointment with this organization and move on. And I almost did.

However, a short time later, I got an appointment with her boss, who invited her—the very person who had hung up on me—to a teleconference.

When I found out that she had been invited to the teleconference, I wondered if I would get hung up on again. Perhaps I had set myself up for another harsh rejection.

But this time there was no rudeness. She could not hang up on me, and she listened politely throughout the entire meeting. "I guess it is a bit hard for her to reject me when her boss asked her to attend," I thought to myself. It took almost all I had not to laugh.

Aim High

Water flows downhill—so does influence. As my experience demonstrates, people have a tendency to be more respectful and compliant when the one making the request is a superior rather than an outside salesperson.

When I first started selling to organizations I would call on mid-level managers, as I thought they were the ones that should handle what I was selling. This sounds reasonable, doesn't it? However, it was common to get a disinterested or even irritated response when calling these mid-level managers. Later, I learned to go higher—to the top of the organization. Often, these top-level people (or their gatekeepers) would direct me to speak to their mid-level managers. I was stunned to see how the mid-level managers now treated me with greater respect because the boss or the gatekeeper of the boss had assigned them to speak with me. "How much time would you like to present?" they would ask politely. Sometimes I would reply that I needed as much as an hour. They would promptly agree. Contrast this to the many times I was not able to get even five minutes when I made a cold call directly to the mid-level manager.

The bad news about complex organizations: They are made up of a lot of people.

This may challenge your ability to find out who the real decision makers are and where the real decision-making power lies.

The good news about complex organizations: They are made up of a lot of people.

A rejection or put off by one person does not mean you are rejected. I believe that there is a way to sell to any organization, even if someone at the organization has rejected you before.

In business-to-business sales, the initial goal is to get in front of a key decision maker. At the beginning, you may not know who carries that decision-making power for the company, and approaching a huge organization without a referral can be intimidating. An inexperienced salesperson may start out by going to someone relatively low on the corporate totem pole. A sales rep or manager can be easier to approach than a director or CEO. But in many cases, you will have greater success by going higher than you need—even to the very top.

Though in large and complex organizations you may not be able to speak to the top-level person on your first call, it is still worth it to try. In one instance, I remember calling an organization and asking to speak with the top person. I was able, on the first cold call, to present a full sales presentation. Admittedly, this isn't always or even often the case. In fact, on many occasions, especially with highly-guarded top people, you should expect that it will take more than one outreach to get an appointment. However, I do believe I would not have presented to the top decision maker that day if I had been too afraid to ask to speak to the top person.

You may get lucky and get an audience with the president, though it isn't likely the president will take the time to listen to your sales pitch. However, she may personally direct you to someone else who deals with your product or service. She will know better than anyone who that is. A referral from the president (or other top person) can have a huge effect on the attitude of the person assigned to hear your presentation.

It is very possible and perhaps even probable that the top person's gatekeeper will send you down a level and refer you to a mid-level manager without even letting you speak to the top person. Though not as ideal as speaking to the top person, it is still a good position to be in. The gatekeeper of the boss is highly influential, and a referral from her will still have a positive impact on how you are treated by the mid-level manager.

The point is that if you can't talk to the top person, you at least want someone higher up to assign someone to speak to you. Whether you start off selling to the top person or whether he assigns you to speak to someone else, most of the time it pays to start at the top.

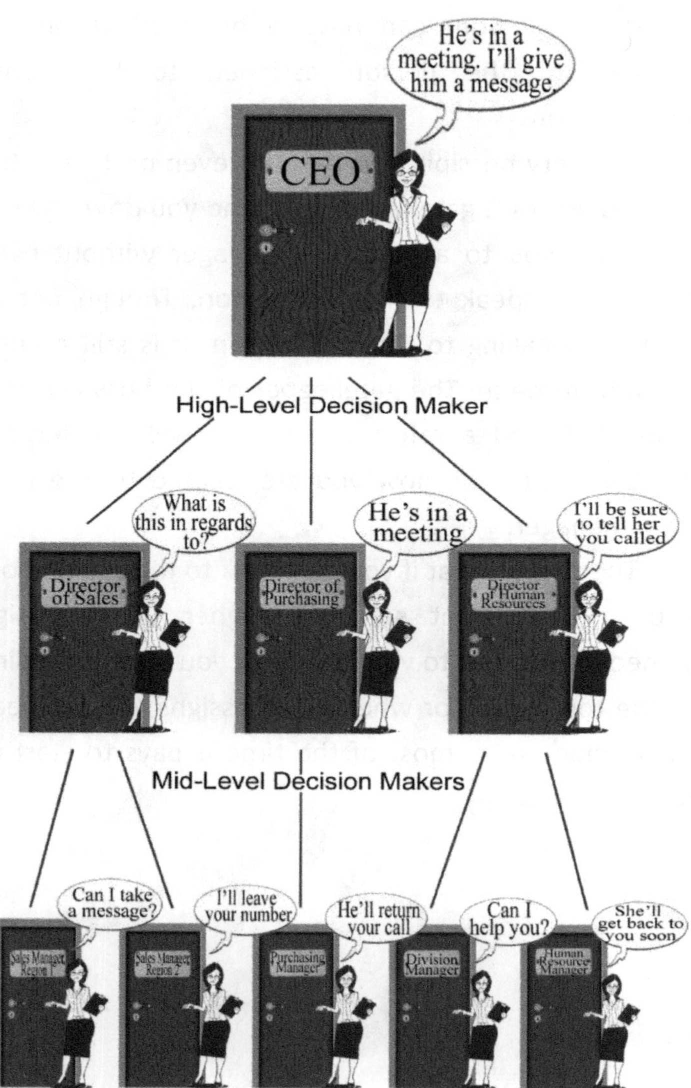

Getting past the "gatekeepers":
receptionist, assistant, executive assistant

Organizations are structured in many different ways. They may be shaped like a pyramid, be "flat", or have a structure entirely unique to the organization. In this book, I will refer to those with high levels of authority and decision-making ability as being at the "top" of the organization regardless of the structure. That top person may be a CEO, a managing director, a president, or use any of a number of different titles.

In most sizable organizations, those who can make significant decisions are generally guarded by at least one "gatekeeper" of some sort. This gatekeeper may have any of a number of different official titles. She may be called a receptionist, an executive assistant, an administrative assistant, or something else entirely. Regardless of the specific title, the gatekeeper will almost always have the responsibility of screening who can and cannot speak with the decision maker. (Generally, unless the gatekeeper has been instructed that the company is in need of a particular service, salespeople are at the bottom of the priority list for the decision maker, and most gatekeepers are used to screening out many if not most sales calls.)

Below the high-level decision makers there are likely mid- and low-level decision makers who may also be guarded by other gatekeepers. For example, if I am calling on a sales organization, I may have a CEO (high-level decision maker) who oversees a director of sales (higher- or mid-level decision maker) who oversees one or several sales managers (mid- or lower-level decision makers).

In a large organization, the CEO, the director of sales, and the sales managers may each have a separate gatekeeper who screens out who can speak to them. In smaller organizations, it is possible that one gatekeeper may "guard" more than one decision maker. There may even be a "switchboard operator" (who may also be known as a receptionist or other title) whose job is to find out what you need and then transfer you to the appropriate person. When you are transferred, you may find that your target is guarded by yet another gatekeeper. In this situation, you now have an outside gatekeeper (the switchboard operator) and more inside gatekeepers (secretaries or assistants to high-, mid-, or lower-level decision makers).

When calling organizations, it is critical that you "make a map" by keeping a record of who is who. Make sure that your records clearly note names, titles, your personal impressions, and which gatekeeper protects which decision maker. (See Chapter Three.)

Sell to the People who can Actually Make Decisions

When I first started selling, I was thrilled to speak with just about anyone, whether or not they had ultimate decision-making power. I quickly learned that if I presented to someone who was not a decision maker, I wasn't going to make a sale. I could get the non-decision makers to salivate over my product or service but they couldn't do anything about it. It doesn't matter that the sales manager loves your product if the vice president of sales is the one that makes the financial decisions. It doesn't matter that the husband says yes if the wife controls the checkbook. I can give a fantastic presentation to the manager, but if she turns around and gives her boss the watered-down version, the boss is unconvinced and the sale is shot.

It doesn't matter how great your presentation or product is if you are selling to the wrong people.

Additionally, I found that in many situations, decisions are made by more than one person. Sometimes decision makers won't make decisions without a buy-in from a director heading the division that handles your type of inquiry.

Uncovering the identity of the key decision maker can be somewhat of a trick. You play the role of detective, sleuthing out clues about who has the ultimate decision-making power and who are the influencers.

To begin, do your research. The company's website is a great place to start when you are looking for the names and contact information of the top individuals when preparing for your initial call. Organizations generally have a structure that has specific lines of authority; these lines of authority are often drawn out on an organizational chart, which may be available on the company's website. (Beware! I have seen some salespeople spend way too much time "researching" an organization online, when what they were really doing was avoiding actually making calls.)

If organizational structure and individual contact information are not available online, start by calling the front office and asking questions. Then listen. Very likely the gatekeeper will open up about who should handle your type of inquiries. It may take multiple calls, but you should be able to find and get a hold of the decision maker.

When you are conducting your research or in contact with the company, realize that there are people within organizations that may have more real influence than their official title lets on. They may have more real influence than people with a more influential title. These people, though not necessarily the decision makers on paper, are oftentimes the real decision makers or, at least, quite influential. It is your job as a salesperson to listen carefully to each interaction so that you can start making an organizational chart or map of who the decision makers are (whether they have the title or not) and start trying to get an appointment with them. You need to investigate who has the real power to make decisions. This information usually comes through building relationships with the gatekeepers and asking questions.

A Process, Not an Event

It is critical to realize that getting an appointment with the appropriate decision makers within an organization is generally not a one-time call or event. More often it is a process that may take a couple of days, weeks, or even several months. It is possible for you to get an appointment on the first call. However, it is also possible that the decision maker is so heavily guarded and scheduled that you will have to differentiate yourself before you will get an appointment (more about this in later chapters). In my experience, I believe most salespeople give up much too early when trying to get an appointment.

An unsuccessful salesperson will take a rejection at face value, be satisfied with the attempt, and move on to the next organization. A successful salesperson will usually stay on the phone longer and continue to gather information, even when transferred a few times. He will later make additional calls, send more emails, and mail more thank you cards as the process continues.

It doesn't matter if the first person says no. One "no" answer does not constitute a rejection. It may take two, three, or even a dozen calls to that decision-making group, so make every call count. Get as much information as you can and as many names as you can, listening carefully and noting everything, so that with each call you are more prepared. It is a process. Use all your resources in each call, and go in with the objective to positively differentiate yourself to people close to the decision maker. Realize that you may have to be patient and persistent to get through. Even if an organization does ultimately turn you down, you may be able to get a referral from them that could lead to another good contact.

How do you leave that positive impression that distinguishes you from all the other salespeople calling in? Good question. Read on . . .

Chapter Two

Treat Gatekeepers Like Gold

I have people call me all day long about your product, and you are the first person that I let into my office about this, and it was because you were nice to my secretary," said Burt, a high-level director at a sizeable organization. "I talk to my secretary more than my family, and some salespeople don't understand that."

I was flabbergasted to learn I was the first person that he had actually met with to discuss my type of product. Competition was fierce in this market, and he had now confirmed that others had wanted to talk to him about it, but he had not been willing to speak with them.

We'll come back to the story of Burt later. But first, let me tell you how I discovered the principle behind how I got an appointment with Burt in the first place.

It all started years before with a visit to the bank. The employee who helped me was very professional and helpful and spent quite a bit of time trying to get a troubling issue resolved for me. After all his time and effort, I said, "I would like to get the email address of your boss so that I can tell him how professional and helpful you have been."

He looked at me in surprise. It was clear from the way he reacted that he was used to handling complaints and negative situations rather than handling people who wanted to compliment him, especially to his boss. Later, I wrote an email to his boss and mentioned that this employee should be recognized and that he was an asset to the company. I copied the email to the employee that had helped me.

A while later, I visited the same branch and was surprised at what happened. I was standing at the back of a line with several other people waiting for the next available teller when a bank employee approached me.

"Mr. Anderson, can I help you with something?" the bank employee asked.

"Yes," I said, a bit surprised. It was not typical to be approached by a banker while at the back of the line. On top of that, I did not recognize this employee, but it was clear that he recognized me.

The bank employee then escorted me from the back of the line, took me to his desk, and allowed me to handle my banking business before several people that were ahead of me in line. I had been to this branch a number of times before and had not been treated like this. Though surprised, I felt like I was one of their very special banking customers.

It didn't stop there. I was treated similarly by other bank employees (most of whom I had never worked with before) not just the employee who was the subject of my email. On more than one occasion, they would recognize me, call me by name, and let me get my banking done ahead of other customers.

What I discovered, almost by accident, was how the principles of positive reinforcement and recognition work. Positive reinforcement is simply creating a positive consequence when someone does something that you want them to do. In short, it is rewarding good behavior. Positive reinforcement works best when the positive consequence comes immediately after the good behavior. Of course, I had heard and read about positive reinforcement, but now I was actually noticing its effects in real life. I had recognized a bank employee who helped me, and now

I was being treated as a VIP whenever I visited that branch.

People like to be acknowledged and recognized.

It is easy for people to complain, and rude demands seem evermore commonplace. When someone takes the time to compliment others, especially to someone who has as much influence over their lives as does their boss, it is like a breath of fresh air.

Now, back to the story about the high-level executive, Burt . . .

A few weeks prior, I had made a cold-call to speak with him. As is almost always the case when calling high-level executives, I was told that he was unavailable. I mentioned to his gatekeeper that I had sent an email to him (more about emails in Chapter Four) and wondered if I could resend it but copy it to her as well "to make sure that he gets it." She agreed to this.

At the end of the call, I said to his gatekeeper, "Thank you, Jane, for helping me. I will mention to Burt that you have been very professional and helpful." She seemed a bit taken off guard, but I could tell that she was pleased.

Then, on the first line of the email that I was resending to her boss, I wrote something like this: "I spoke briefly with Jane. She was very professional and helpful."

I then continued with a short note about how I was resending an email I had sent earlier and that I would appreciate an opportunity to meet.

Again, this email was sent to the high-level director *and* copied to Jane with the first line being a compliment about her. Do you think that Jane had an incentive to show this to her boss?

I had now differentiated myself to Jane from the hundreds of other emails she likely received each month. I was different in her eyes. I cared enough to help her with something *she* cared about—her job. I had treated the "menial" gatekeeper with the same courtesy and respect that I did someone with greater status. When I showed her and her boss that she mattered and positively reinforced her behavior, I came away with the appointment I wanted. I had been granted a presentation when many others were ignored.

That simple, sincere compliment was the key to that gate and many others. The act of being kind to the gatekeeper (someone many salespeople assume has the low job with no importance or leverage) proved to have a great amount of influence, and soon I was in the office, face-to-face with a key decision maker.

I have heard of sales tactics that teach salespeople to act indignant to the gatekeeper to get through and get their way. I disagree with these techniques completely. If I had come into the bank and shown indignation, angrily demanding service, I may have had someone fix the problem in the short run, but in the long run the employees would probably avoid me. Appointments with the right people sometimes take a while to get. Acting indignant in the short run will kill your prospects in the long run. As the saying goes, honey works better than vinegar.

Principle: Everyone is important.

Everyone in sales, and can help you find success in all of life. To treat some people importantly and others as less important is a type of snobbery. When you treat the janitor with the same courtesy and respect as you treat a CEO, you demonstrate true inner character.

"Influential" people are not more important than "non-influential people." In fact, in organizations the "non-decision makers" are often the ones that eventually help the decision makers actually make the decision. In many situations, it is the gatekeeper who really runs the show. He reminds the boss where she needs to be and when, books her schedule, screens her phone calls, etc. The gatekeeper may even be the one who actually makes the decision regarding your product or service despite not having the official title. Gatekeepers often act as trusted advisors to the people they guard. Often gatekeepers and decision makers are very close.

Acknowledgement and Recognition

Billions of dollars are spent each year on recognizing noteworthy performers. Does that number seem high? Think company incentive trips and prizes. Think the Oscars! Praise and recognition go a long way, and they can go a long way in helping your business.

Acknowledging and recognizing a gatekeeper effectively is a three-step process:

1. Find something that you can honestly and *sincerely* compliment her on.
2. Write a note to the decision maker or boss.
3. Copy the gatekeeper on the email.

These simple steps can do wonders for your appointment-setting process, perhaps more than anything else. Through them, you are positively distinguishing yourself from all other salespeople to both the gatekeeper and the decision maker—essentially unlocking the gate.

Remember, the principle of recognizing others is timeless. Even if email was replaced by some other form of communication, you could still use the principle of recognition in your sales endeavors, and I believe strongly that it would still be effective.

Again, be sincere and honest. Most gatekeepers of high-level executives are very professional, helpful, and polite—that is why they are gatekeepers of high-level people. Thus, it shouldn't be hard to sincerely find something positive about the gatekeeper to relate to her boss. Let the gatekeeper know you will be praising her in the email so she will be looking for it.

(Note: If the gatekeeper is not professional and helpful, which occasionally is the case, don't compliment her. *The compliment must be sincere and honest.* There have been times when I have chosen not to compliment a gatekeeper when her conduct did not merit it.)

Positive reinforcement is not a new concept. In my study of psychology, I was fascinated to find that positive reinforcement is much more effective than punishment or negative reinforcement.

For example, when conditioning an animal to perform a task such as pushing a lever, the trainer waits until the animal actually performs the task and then rewards it with food or something else to immediately reinforce the behavior that the trainer wishes to see. Doing this increases the chance that the animal will perform the behavior again.

Please know that I am not suggesting that animals and people are on the same level. However, people react to positive reinforcement in much the same way. When a gatekeeper says that it is OK to resend an email and copy it to her, she is moving (even if very slightly) in the direction you want (i.e. helping you) and she needs to be immediately and sincerely reinforced. Reinforcing her when she helps you greatly increases the chance that she will help you again.

Again, using recognition to help you set an appointment is a simple process: sincerely compliment the gatekeeper to her boss, copy her on the email, and send it either while still on the call or within minutes of finishing the call (the sooner the better). The reason that you want to do it soon is that you want her to associate the positive feelings with you. Remember, positive reinforcement works best when you *immediately* reinforce the desired behavior. There is no need to be overly lavish. A simple compliment like, "she was very courteous and professional" or, "he was very polite and helpful" is all you need.

I have noticed a considerable difference in the gatekeeper's friendliness and willingness to help me get an appointment with the decision maker after doing this. Generally, when I call back later to follow up, the gatekeeper is very friendly and super polite. Often, she will go out of her way to persuade the decision maker to make an appointment with me.

Later, when the gatekeeper gets you an appointment, a real thank you card (hand-written) is appropriate:

"Thank you for taking the time to assist me recently. I know you are busy, and I really appreciated it."

No hints about setting up a follow-up appointment. No pitches for your product. No "I hope we can do business." Just a simple, unfeigned thank you card.

Another thank you card should go to the person or people you had the appointment with as well (more about thank you cards in a later chapter).

The principle is that everyone matters—everyone. One possible technique that arises from this principle is to acknowledge and reinforce "non-decision makers," sincerely finding something to compliment the gatekeeper about to her boss. Another technique is to quickly send a thank you card or email (or both) to a gatekeeper after *any* positive interaction.

What other ways can you positively reinforce behaviors when people help you during the sales process? If you truly understand the principle, your imagination and creativity may help you come up with many new techniques.

Love is the Answer

This may sound quaint, humorous, or even offensive to some seasoned, more jaded salespeople, but the truth is that "Love is the Answer." Love melts defenses. When you choose to truly care about the person on the other end of the line, he or she will sense it. That's why complimenting the secretary to the boss works. If you are trying to manipulate, she will sense it. You may ask, "How can I care about someone I just met?" The answer is simple. You choose to. It is simply a choice. You have to be genuinely interested in helping the gatekeeper. You have to care enough to truly listen, not just selectively listen, or pretend you are listening. Listen. Really listen. Be brave enough to love the person on the other end of the line. This is a person just like you. A person who has real dreams, real fears, has experienced disappointment, and who feels deeply just like you and me. Be willing to do something to truly help her, whether or not she gets you the appointment.

Chapter Three

Personal Touch

There are thousands of salespeople out there who are trying to get appointments with key decision makers. Many of them are successful. Perhaps even more are not. What makes the difference? Both successful and unsuccessful salespeople are making calls. Both are sending emails. Why are some successful and others not? Is it a difference of talent and experience? Those may be contributing factors, but there are actions that can augment (or perhaps compensate for lack of) talent and experience. Indeed, there are small gestures and techniques that make the big difference between success and failure.

One Little Thank You Card

Some time ago, I gave a solid presentation to key decision makers at an organization. They reacted positively, and I thought that they would buy. After the presentation, however, they seemed to drop off the face of the earth. I called and emailed and there was no response. I called again and emailed again. Nothing. I waited and waited and called some more. Then I waited. Still nothing. Weeks passed. I started to think that perhaps they would not buy and that I had missed something during the sales process.

I then decided to send a simple thank you card. The card did not try to pitch anything. It did not say, "We look forward to having your business." It was simple, direct, and thanked the main decision maker for speaking with me. It was sent through the mail on a real card—not emailed. It wasn't long before I had an email from the decision maker wanting to move forward. The next time we spoke, she was quick to thank me for the card.

Technology is changing and evolving at a breathtaking pace. Advertisers promote each new tool or social media avenue as the "magic bullet" to increase sales. They often forget one really important factor: people. Human nature is basically the same even if technology has changed. In fact, we still need and may even crave human attention more than we did earlier because of technology. Instead of truly connecting us, there is much of technology that tends to isolate us.

I recently visited the campus of a major university and was surprised at how many of the students had earphones in their ears, probably listening to music rather than conversing with each other. It was strikingly quiet. Here were large numbers of students *not* communicating, just stuck in their own little world, wires coming out of their ears.

Reach out. Communicate. Connect in real, tangible ways. Real people, including gatekeepers, are hungry for real communication and connection. One of the best moves you can make when setting appointments is to send cards or thank you notes to people; this includes both decision makers and gatekeepers and anyone else you may have spoken to. Keep a box of cards and stamps on hand or use an online card service, and make it a habit to send thank you cards.

Remember, gatekeepers work hard and may not get all the recognition they expect or feel they deserve. When they are acknowledged, they often are very grateful for the recognition they receive. With the gatekeeper on your side, you may be surprised at how influential he can be in helping you get an appointment with the right people.

Power of Reciprocity

People are hard-wired to reciprocate good for good or favor for favor. When a couple invites you to a party, you will invite them to yours in return. When your neighbor brings you cookies, chances are you will soon be warming up your oven to send some homemade bread their way. We feel a need to return what someone else has provided us. It may be out of obligation or sincere desire to return the kindness, but whatever our reason, we do it.

A professor once conducted an experiment on this concept, the results of which were published in *Social Science Research* in 1976. He sent out Christmas cards to complete strangers. He expected some reaction, but a short time later, Christmas cards came pouring in from many of those strangers—people who had never met or heard of him. Many just replied to the return address with a Christmas card.[1] Imagine the conversation on the other end:

"Honey, I got this Christmas card in the mail today. Do you recognize him?"

"No. Don't you? Ah, well, we should probably send him one. Add him to the list."

Gatekeepers respond to the idea of reciprocity as well. When you treat them kindly, offer a compliment to the boss, and send a thank you card, human nature nudges them to return the favor by helping you get an appointment.

As a former gatekeeper herself, my wife remembers salespeople who would come in and treat her with kindness. She would make an extra effort to ensure they had time with the decision makers, put in a good word for them, and even push for their business when she could. Years later, she still remembers their names and faces because they built a relationship of trust and left positive impressions during their interactions with her.

Noting Details

People like to feel important and remembered. This is especially true of gatekeepers, who may feel like they are the glue that holds the company together but are seldom recognized for their efforts. Remembering "little" details about the gatekeeper may help you build rapport and melt the defenses that gatekeepers tend to deploy when screening out salespeople. You move from a faceless, pushy salesperson into an acquaintance they look forward to speaking with. With this elevated level of connection, you are more likely to get through the "gate" to the decision maker.

Remembering seemingly unimportant details about people often makes a huge difference later in the sales process. People love to be remembered and known, so when you recall significant or even minor details about them, they feel important and cared about. On a follow-up call, if you talk about details shared in previous conversations, a connection is made and rapport is built. If you note the exact way words were used, in future calls you can build rapport by using the person's vernacular.

I once had a conversation with a gatekeeper who mentioned that her husband was from Scandinavia. I had actually lived in Scandinavia for a couple of years myself, so we had a nice conversation about her husband's home country. I made a note about his background and our conversation so that when I called back, I could casually ask if they had any plans for going to Scandinavia or something else that would let her know that I had remembered her. Later when I spoke to her I mentioned Scandinavia, and I could tell that there was an immediate connection and trust.

Another time, I spoke with a prospect who had recently been in the hospital due to an unexpected illness. Because I noted it, I was able to casually mention that I knew he had been in the hospital and ask him how he was feeling. He instantly knew I cared about him, that he was not just someone I was trying to work to get the sale. He opened up about his experience and went on and on while I simply listened. His willingness to talk as well as my willingness to listen helped take the relationship further. With the hundreds of conversations I have monthly, if I hadn't made a few brief notes about his hospital visit, I might not have remembered that important event in his life, and he probably would not have opened up to me the way he did.

When calling on potential prospects, it is possible to make hundreds of new contacts every week, and it is impossible to remember detailed information about each one. That's where taking good notes comes into play. The more specific the notes the better. You should make detailed notes following and sometimes during *every* conversation. Notes help you remember the small things that are important to the prospects and let them know they are important to you.

Following the first call when you have complimented the gatekeeper to her boss, you may find the gatekeeper is often very friendly. You may start to chit chat. No matter what she says, you should note it so you can bring it up again later. Record even seemingly minor details. Mirror words and vernacular to help you seem more connected. We like people who are similar to us. Using the phrase "cold spell" like she did instead of “storm” when recalling their recent weather bout can help you connect more to her. If a secretary repeatedly refers to her husband as "Fred" instead of "my husband" you should also refer to him as "Fred" even though you don't know him. On the other hand, if she refers to her husband as "my husband" you should refer to him as "your husband" and not "Fred." Also, make note of your impressions, as they may prove to be valuable resources when calling back.

If you are not listening carefully or paying close attention, you will miss things. The gatekeeper might randomly throw out information that could prove beneficial later on. I once called a prospect who mentioned that her sewing machine was broken and she needed to buy a new one. I noted that detail, and the next time I spoke with her, I asked about her sewing machine. She couldn't believe I remembered. You never know what minor detail will help you in the future, so make a note of *everything* that is said. If the gatekeeper mentions that the decision maker is away at a conference, write it down. Later when you speak with the decision maker you can bring it up: "You've been busy lately. Don't you love those conferences?"

Sometimes the little, seemingly unimportant things that you make note of are the things that will help most in getting you the appointment.

You should be taking notes specifically about the people that you talk to, including their title and what you spoke about. Little details are very helpful, especially in large organizations. It does not matter if you use a notebook, CRM (customer relationship management) software, or online service. (As I write this, there are a number of reputable "cloud" based CRM systems that are relatively easy to figure out and that make note taking quite easy.) Regardless of the system you use, your communications should be noted in a way that you can easily see what happened recently and maintain a brief history of your last notes. Ideally, your notes or CRM should allow you to see previous interactions at a glance without having to click into or rummage through different pages to see the history of your conversation with a particular prospect or gatekeeper. This efficient way to manage your time will pay big dividends.

Making a Map

It is important to start making a "map" of who is who in a complex/multi-level organization. In essence, you are creating an organization chart that includes first and last names and titles of each person in the company. You can simply make notes of the information or draw it out in a diagram to help you visualize it better. Sometimes you can find an organizational chart for the company on its website. This is a good place to start (but don’t consider it a place to finish, because it isn't). Whatever your method, your map should be detailed, focusing on gatekeepers as well as decision makers. Many, if not most, organization charts don't include gatekeepers. They aren't considered significant enough to include (we know better!).

Your map should include which gatekeeper guards which decision maker and who the real decision makers are. This is especially important in large organizations where there may be multiple levels of gatekeepers as well as groups of people who are tasked with making decisions and where you will need to influence multiple members within the group.

In your map, include specific notes about the organization such as first names, titles, who's who and how they relate to each other, lines of authority, etc.

For example, you may note that Janice is the gatekeeper for Dale and that Charles is the gatekeeper for Susan and that Dale reports to Susan.

Making a map is like heading into an unfamiliar forest in the dark. There is a maze winding through the forest and you have to chart it. You can't see anything, but through taking twists and turns and drawing out each corner and path, by the time you are done you will almost have a bird's eye view of the forest. You will know all the trails that pass through and all the campgrounds and lanes.

Note everything! Specifically ask for information ("Who handles this?"). With each phone transfer, you are getting new names. Use every phone call as an opportunity to build your map. What if the first person you speak with isn't very helpful and transfers you to the wrong person? Take advantage of the situation. The next person may correct the problem and send you to the right person. "I'm sorry. I'm in HR, but who you really need to talk to is Scott in purchasing." You just got more names and titles for your map. Note every single thing. What if the decision maker isn't available (and don't expect that she will be)? Ask to be transferred to the assistant. An unsuccessful salesperson would note that he *tried* to call the decision maker and she was unavailable and move on to the next call. Bad move! Don't stop at *try*. You have to keep going. Get in and get more info. Remember, you are in uncharted territory, and it is your job to map it out.

Having your map readily accessible when making calls to the organization is very helpful so you can recall names of others in the organization quickly and without delay. For example, when you are transferred to a key person in the company, you could mention, "I spoke with Jeanette and Kathy. They both mentioned that you were the person I needed to talk to."

As you are talking to the gatekeeper and mapping out the organization, you are clueing in to first names. Use them! In future phone calls or when speaking with others in the organization, referring to their co-workers by their first names helps you sound like an insider. You may have never spoken to them in your life, but that doesn't matter. They refer to each other by first name, and so should you. You build rapport by talking like they do, and you feel more like an insider to the people you speak with. When you ask for the decision maker by his first name, this says that you have a right to be able to talk to him and that you expect the gatekeeper to transfer the call.

"Hey, Rob. Stephanie and I were just chatting about your golf game. She said it's a passion of yours." Or, "How's it going Heather? I was just talking to Chris and he said Mark was the person I needed to talk to. Is he available?"

Contrast those friendly and casual encounters with this more formal, and less effective, approach: "Hello ma'am. This is Mr. Anderson. I'm trying to reach Mr. Barton to discuss his computer needs with him. Is he available?"

It may seem professional, but psychologically it says "outsider."

I stated earlier that I don't think you need to act indignant to get past gatekeepers—that honey works better than vinegar. I firmly believe this. However, being overly friendly or overly nice can backfire as well. It is important to be polite but sound confident and direct. You should approach the gatekeeper with the *unspoken* confidence and tone-of-voice that says "of course you are going to transfer me to the decision maker" even though you would likely never say this directly. Confidence is key. Remember, much of communication is nonverbal—it's in the tone of voice and body language. In other words, I could give you scripts for what works for me and it still may not work for you, because what you are saying with your tone of voice and your body language may actually ruin what you say. On the other hand, your pitch may be a disaster and you may stumble over your words but still have a very successful sales approach, because your tone of voice and/or your body language make up for it.

The most important thing to remember is that you are dealing with a real person who matters, not just someone who stands in the way of reaching someone more important. The techniques of sending thank you cards, remembering small details, and using first names all help serve one purpose: to establish a personal connection. You become more real to them as they become more real to you. As you sincerely care and use these gestures to show it, you are reaching out with a personal touch that will set you apart.

Chapter Four

Jujitsu Email

Email, ah, email. The safe, conservative way to market. It's so much easier to shoot out a form email than to actually make a phone call. It's also much easier to handle a rejection via email when it's not as personal. In fact, most of the time there isn't a rejection! The email just gets ignored. There is rarely a response for the very reason it is so much easier to email: it's not personal. Even if you write a unique email to each organization you contact, it is still not personal, as it lacks human connection.

The chances of getting an appointment through email are low. If you blast out a lot of emails to a lot of organizations, then the likelihood of getting a "bite" increases, though the percentages are still low. If you are just trying to get in with one specific company and you simply email them and think you did a good job, you need to reconsider your strategy. If you are worried about not getting appointments and all you do is email, that is why you are not getting appointments.

Because it is so easy to send emails, decision makers may receive hundreds of emails a day, and they simply don't have the time or desire to respond to or even read each one. Even the gatekeeper, who may have the job of sorting the Inbox, probably doesn't read them all. Assume your email is as good as SPAM. You become a needle in a haystack, which is why email alone is not enough. But coupled with additional tools, email can be part of a powerful strategy.

Email alone = Weak

Email combined with additional tools = Strong

The main purpose of email is to give you a reason to call. Here's how it works:

You send an initial email to the decision maker. In this email, you can address a problem or challenge the company may need help resolving, and you may also include a powerful statement about your company. You are not trying to sell in this email; you are simply trying to set up an appointment. You can let them know briefly what your company does, but keep it to that. You need to first understand the needs of the company before you begin selling your product or service, so that you can tailor your position to them. Leave the selling to the actual appointment.

You craft a simple, concise email and shoot it off to join the hundreds of other emails in the decision maker's inbox. A few days later, you call and ask for the decision maker.

This sets the gatekeeper up to mention that the decision maker is unavailable, which is almost always the case and is what you expect and are prepared for. It also sets you up perfectly to resend the email, but this time you will copy it to her and, if she has been helpful and courteous, compliment her to her boss.

You: May I speak with Shawn please?

Gatekeeper: Shawn is not in right now. May I ask who is calling?

You: This is Mark with Gicklegak, Inc. I sent an email to Shawn a few days ago, and I am following up on that email. (Notice that I call the decision maker by his first name to build rapport.)

Gatekeeper: Shawn is unavailable right now. He is at a leadership conference. (Note this detail.)

You: Hmm. Good for him. Maybe what I can do is resend the email to him. Oh, and do you mind if I copy you on it? Just to make sure he gets it?

Gatekeeper: That's fine.

You: What's the best email address for you?

Gatekeeper: My email is ____________.

You: (repeating back the email) Is that right?

Gatekeeper: You got it.

You: Great. I'll send that email right now. By the way, you have been very helpful and professional. Really, I speak to a lot of people every day, and I really appreciate your courteous manner. I will make sure to mention that to Shawn in the email. (Again, the way you say it is more important than what you say. Also, it must be sincere.)

Gatekeeper: Really? Thank you.

You: Of course. I'll send it over right now, and if you could make sure he gets it, that would be great. And then if you could, give me a call or email me a time when he can meet. I'm sure that he is very busy. You can let him know that I will try to be flexible with his schedule.

Gatekeeper: I will. Thanks.

You: (pausing slightly as you finish typing) I just resent the email. Did you get it?

Gatekeeper: Let me check. Yes, I got it. Thank you again for the compliment.

You: (Sincerely) Well, I really appreciated your helpfulness.

Gatekeeper: I will talk to him when he gets back and let you know.

You: Thank you. I look forward to hearing back from you.

(It should be noted here that you simply resent the email you had sent earlier, but this time you copied it to the gatekeeper with a compliment:

TO: Shawn@__________.org

CC: Sheila@__________.org

Dear Shawn:

I spoke briefly with Sheila. She was very courteous and helpful.

I am resending an email that I had sent earlier. I will be in your area on Tuesday and Thursday of next week. Will one of those days work to meet?

Mark

(This, of course, is followed by the text from your original email.)

At this point, if you didn't do it on the call, immediately resend the email to the decision maker and copy it to the gatekeeper. She now has an incentive to make sure her boss sees your email—you've made it important to her career. This is the same email that only a few minutes before was buried in the Inbox. You have now positively differentiated yourself and made great distance on the path to your appointment.

Jujitsu Emails

Jujitsu is an ancient Japanese fighting technique that uses skill to outmaneuver the opponent. It is the art of using people's weight and momentum against them. If I am 150 pounds and a 330 pound, solid guy is charging me, the outcome doesn't look very promising for me. However, if I can use his 330 pounds of force against him by tripping him or getting out of the way of his momentum where he can't stop, I can use my smallness to my advantage and his bigness to his disadvantage.

The same principle can be applied in your email approach. I play win-win, so I'm not suggesting that the organization is your opponent. Quite the contrary.

They are on your side, and you are on theirs. Instead, I'm suggesting that you use the organization's internal strengths and relationships to make your way into the company. Central to this is establishing a good relationship with the top person's gatekeeper.

Let's say you follow my recommendation to start at the top. In a large organization, the top person may not be the person you need to speak to. Even knowing this, you email the top-level person (or at least someone high up in the company) and then call his gatekeeper later to follow up on the email. When she informs you that you need to contact someone down a level or two, ask her if she would forward your email to the correct person and copy it to you. I have found that most gatekeepers are happy to do this, especially if you have treated them like gold (see Chapter Two). When she is the one forwarding your email, you not only have the information for your new contact but, more importantly, you are using jujitsu.

I have mentioned several times that the top person's gatekeeper has a significant amount of influence: she is his right-hand person and often his eyes and ears. When the top person's gatekeeper forwards your email, it suddenly carries much more weight and is much more powerful because it comes from the top rather than from an unknown, outside salesperson. You are using the internal structure and corporate hierarchy to your advantage. Your email is now taken seriously.

Once your email has been forwarded to the appropriate person, any further communication should be copied to the original, high-level gatekeeper. This does two things:

1. It keeps the gatekeeper, a key influencer inside the organization, informed about what is going on so she can assist you.
2. It quietly reminds the mid- or lower-level personnel (who can see that the email has been copied to the high-level gatekeeper) that the high-level person is encouraging them to meet with you.

In a successful sales approach process, it is likely that your email will eventually get passed along to at least a few, if not many, people. Having influential names in the organization attached to your email message will give you great momentum to jujitsu your way to an appointment.

Crafting the Email

As stated earlier, an email alone is unlikely to garner a lot of sales or attention without some follow-up calls and/or other interactions. However, once the sales process moves along, the email very likely will be passed around to others and therefore should meet the following criteria:

1. It should be well written with no spelling or grammar errors. Many top-level people and their secretaries can easily spot grammar, syntax, and spelling errors and may make assumptions about your intelligence or education. It can be a deal-breaker if your email is riddled with mistakes. In today's world of texts and tweets, many people now think that grammar, punctuation, and proper capitalization are not important; on the contrary, correct grammar is essential, especially in your initial email.

2. It should be written to a well-educated audience, meeting the level of your general reader. This doesn't mean that you should add a lot of complicated words; it just means that you should mirror their writing style. For example, referencing industry-specific words or phrases may help them understand that you know where they are coming from.

3. It should be friendly. Written word is only a small part of communication. Tone and body language make up a significant part, all of which are lacking in writing. On email you may have to be a little nicer to compensate for not being able to look them in the eye and smile. If you have to error on being overly nice or not, be overly nice. You want to make it completely clear it is friendly so they don't interpret it differently.

4. It should address a problem that the company or industry likely faces. Without talking to them, you may not know their exact challenges; however, often your target sales group may share many of the same challenges. If you have been able to help other organizations with these challenges, mention that.

5. It should include a direct invitation to meet or speak with them.

6. It should be brief and concise. Most decision makers want to be able to scan an email quickly. They don't want a book. If it would take more than three-fourths of a page to print out with a normal font, then it is probably too long. Remember, the email is supposed to get them interested to meet, *not* sell your product or service.

Chapter Five

Integrity and the Dog Chasing Phenomenon

Imagine you were listening in on my conversation with a potential customer and you heard me say one or more of the following statements:

"Our solution may not be the best alternative for your company."

"What we have might not even be something that you need."

"Our product may not be the best fit for your company, and if it isn't, we don't want you do to business with us."

"This product may not be right for you."

You would probably question my competency as a salesman and maybe even question my sanity. You may be afraid that by making suggestions like those above, my potential customers would agree with the statement, and that would be the end of the conversation.

Wrong.

In fact, I believe that saying the above statements (or something similar) at the right time would actually increase my chances of getting an appointment or sale, and they can do the same for you.

There are three reasons for this:

First, you are breaking their psychological pattern. You are defying your potential customer's or the gatekeeper's expectations by acting *nothing* like the stereotypical salesperson, which breaks down their natural defensiveness. You can't defend when there is nothing to defend against. Saying, "this might not be for you" is what they are already thinking, so they don't need to defend against it.

I teach negotiation and sales techniques and principles to salespeople. In my classes, I ask why salespeople are disliked, or at the least avoided, by many. They often reply that many people think of salespeople as dishonest, pushy, manipulative, willing to say anything to get the sale, caring only about their commissions.

Unfortunately, this is a widely-held viewpoint. Some less-than-scrupulous, pushy, and overly aggressive salespeople have given a bad name to our noble profession.

In order to counter that reputation and positively distinguish yourself from others, you must act exactly opposite of everything that gives salespeople a bad name. In other words, you must be willing to be *confident* enough to be honest, non-pushy, and non-manipulative. Say the opposite of what they expect from a pushy salesperson. Instead, act more like a friend.

The best salespeople are the best salespeople because they act nothing like a stereotypical salesperson.

When we genuinely treat our customers as we do our friends, we are there with information and support, but we do not pressure them into the sale. When we sense apprehension, we don't push. We converse and mirror their feelings. We help them see the benefits of our product or service, but we do not pressure them to make a decision in our favor; sometimes we even help them see that a different product would be better for them. We step back and allow them ownership of their decision. This lack of pressure is a vital component in a friendship.

Ironically, the less like a typical salesperson you are, the more sales you will make. Once again, being pushy, aggressive, and dishonest will *not* get you as many sales as being honest, non-pushy, and just acting like a friend who wants to help. Taken one step further, mildly trying to talk the prospect out of getting an appointment with you may make them want to listen to you more.

Principle: Act with integrity.

Second, the statements at the beginning of this chapter are probably honest. The truth is that your product or service may not really be the best alternative or the best solution for their company. The truth is that it really may not be a good fit between your product or service and their company. The truth is that you don't know yet because you haven't had the time to discuss and truly find out what the company and the decision makers need. You haven't taken the time to understand their vision for the company. By caring for the customer's real needs above your own commission, you are showing integrity. If your integrity is genuine, you don't want to sell them a product that won't really help.

Think of the Santa Claus in the classic movie Miracle on 34th Street. Originally, he had been instructed to lead children to ask for toys that could be found in their department store. But instead, when a child sat on his lap and asked for a toy the store did not carry, Santa told the child's mother the toy could be purchased at a competing store. She was surprised to hear this, to which Santa replied that the children's happiness was most important. The mother located the manager and let him know that she was so impressed by the way things were handled that she would now be a regular customer.[2]

The best part is that it wasn't a ploy or marketing stunt (at least at first). Santa had an honest intent to help the customer, and his sincerity ultimately increased sales. Keep in mind, when you tell a customer to look elsewhere, the statement must be genuine to be effective. Quoting a scripted line simply to get the sale is manipulative—right back in typical salesperson mode. Also, if everyone starts using my exact lines, they will lose their effectiveness. People will begin to expect the salesperson to ask if the product is really right for them. That is why technique alone is not enough. You need the principle of integrity and genuine personal sincerity to find success using these methods.

Because you are telling the truth and because the prospect is likely already thinking at some level that your product is not for them, you build rapport when you show understanding by saying, "Our product may not be right for you." By telling the truth and acting differently than most salespeople, you don't have to say, "Trust me and relax." Your actions allow them to do just that: trust you and relax.

Third, the statements at the beginning of the chapter coincide with what I call the Dog Chasing Phenomenon. Have you ever noticed that if you chase a dog it will run, but if you run the dog chases you? Now, I am the first to acknowledge that people are not dogs and that generalizing about humans and dogs may be considered a stretch. However, when we as salespeople get too intense and "chase" our prospects, they can sense our insecurity and intensity and will generally back away. On the other hand, when we are confident and honest enough to suggest things that most salespeople would not, such as the fact that our product may not be right for them, we are figuratively "running" or at least stepping back. This allows them to "chase" us. I cannot tell you how many times I could sense that a prospect or gatekeeper was a bit apprehensive, and instead of pushing for the appointment, I would pull back a bit or run, which in turn led them to pull themselves in or chase me.

When you confidently acknowledge their concerns and suggest that your product or service may not be right for them, you provide an "out" and remove the pressure. The gatekeeper or decision maker can let their guard down and relax because the stress of possibly having to reject you is lessened. Most people have difficulty rejecting salespeople, and it is likely that the thought of rejecting you stresses them out. When they relax, your chances of getting an appointment or taking the sale to the next level increase dramatically.

Principle: Act with Integrity

Honesty and integrity are timeless principles.
When we tell the truth, we are trusted.
Telling the truth does a number of things:
A) It makes you feel good, relaxed, and at ease because you are aligning yourself with a timeless principle.
B) It increases the chances that the prospect or gatekeeper will feel good, relaxed, and at ease (because you don't seem to be like all of the other pushy, dishonest salespeople who will say anything to get a sale).
C) Consciously or unconsciously, people will feel that they can trust you. They may not even be able to articulate why they feel they can trust you, but the feeling will be there.

When I first started out in sales, I went door-to-door. I found that if I "chased" my prospect by being excited and intense, people would often push back by slamming the door in my face. I learned to try the reverse approach. Instead of being intense I had to be very calm. Instead of being excited I had to be very relaxed. My new tactic was to stand mostly facing away when people answered the door and to let the other person speak first. Those small gestures helped break the prospects' psychological pattern and kept them from seeing me as a typical, pushy salesperson.

"Can I help you?" they would ask, wondering why I was standing on their porch and saying nothing.

Turning around very calmly and slowly I would say, "I know I'm probably the last person you want to see on your doorstep, and you probably aren't even interested in what I have to say." This statement was true and *not* what a typical salesperson would normally say. Truthfully, for most people, a door-to-door salesperson is one of the last people they would like to see. Also, statistically, most people aren't interested, so by saying, "You probably aren't even interested in what I have to say," I was telling the truth. I noticed that people were generally much more relaxed and willing to speak to me when I used this approach than when I was acting in an excited, intense, chasing manner.

"Well, what do you have to say?" they would ask.

My body language and my non-salesy approach had broken their expectation of the typical salesperson, and now they were asking *me* what I had to say. I was figuratively running, and they were chasing. I would explain why I was there, making sure that I was calm and relaxed. It might have almost seemed like I didn't care if they bought from me. This attitude of not caring actually made it easier for them to care and chase me. My tactics might not seem like enough to make a difference, but I was consistently among the top producers of any sales teams I was a part of. I even had success selling houses door-to-door (not a product you generally find from a door-to-door salesperson).

Let me give you another example of the dog chasing principle. Sometimes after making a sale, I would take the contract and the check and push it back to my new clients and ask, "Are you sure you want to do this?" Now, many salespeople might be appalled that I would suggest that you ask this question as it seems that I am trying to talk the prospect out of the sale I just made. However, when asking this question sincerely and with confidence, I cannot tell you how many times I would just sit back and try to keep from smiling as I would listen to my new clients tell me all of the reasons why buying my product or service was a good idea. I don't think that I had one person change their mind at that point. In fact, I believe that my low cancellation rate in sales was because I was willing to confidently ask questions like these. They had to chase me rather than me chase them. Also, I wasn't acting like a stereotypical, pushy salesperson, which made them trust me more. I never said, "I am concerned about you and want to help you make a good choice," but the clients could feel it.

However, let's say that the client did bring up a concern or was uneasy about moving forward. It is much better to deal with the concern now than later when they are trying to cancel the sale.

The Dance

Here is another way to think about the psychology of getting appointments. Relationships—even newly formed, cold-calling relationships between prospects and salespeople—are almost like a dance. Imagine a couple dancing together, hand-in-hand, with a bit of distance between them; they are close but not touching. When one of the dance partners moves closer to their partner, the other person then moves in closer as well, coming together. They may even touch in a sort of embrace. A split second later, they may both step apart while still holding hands and continue the dance. The partners are continually moving in and out together, balancing rhythm, closeness, and space.

Salespeople and customers engage in their own form of dance as they navigate the sales or appointment-setting process. When one person, usually the prospect or gatekeeper, steps back, it is appropriate for the other person (usually the salesperson) to step back as well. This gives the prospect or gatekeeper the feeling of safety and space, which makes it possible and more likely that they will continue the relationship. If the same prospect or gatekeeper steps in, the salesperson should respond positively and be compelling. Throughout the fluid process, the salesperson is mirroring the actions of the other person.

For example, when you can sense some apprehension from the gatekeeper or prospect, you should fight the natural tendency to push ahead, and instead you might back off with a statement like, "This may not be for your organization, and if it's not, no big deal. I don't want you to meet with us if it doesn't make sense for you or your group."

Then just pause and say *nothing*. Often, the person will relax and then agree to speak further or even meet because he feels less pressure.

A problem occurs when you, sensing that the gatekeeper has some apprehension, decide to step closer, and then closer, and then closer still by giving all the reasons that your product or service is amazing or reasons why you believe you should get an appointment with the decision maker. And each time you do this, the gatekeeper figuratively and emotionally backs up and becomes more and more apprehensive, eventually rejecting you altogether. The dance is no longer a dance. It has become a chase, and the gatekeeper is running. The more you chase like a typical salesperson, the more the prospect or gatekeeper runs, and the chances for an appointment dwindle fast. If there is going to be a chase, you want the gatekeeper chasing you, not the other way around.

Not only should you mirror the actions and emotions of the other person, but you should mirror their level of intensity as well. Too often salespeople act like a car sale radio announcer. You know the one. The announcer in a loud, booming voice lets you know he has just the car for you and financing is not an issue. What if you talked to your prospect that way: Chris, HAVE I GOT A DEAL FOR YOU?! BUY NOW, I'VE GOT THE BEST SYSTEM AT THE LOWEST PRICE OF THE YEAR. BAD CREDIT. NO PROBLEM. BANKRUPTCY? NO PROBLEM! Not only would you sound ridiculous but your prospect would do an about-face and run.

Here are a few examples of how the dance and chase could work:

Chase

Gatekeeper: I think that we already have a product that does what you are selling. I don't think we need your product. (Stepping back.)

Salesperson: But I don't think you understand how good our product really is. It beats the competition. It's awesome. I really want to talk to Mike so he can see how much money he is wasting using your current product. (Steps in again and pushes.)

Gatekeeper: Like I said, I think that what we have works just fine. (Stepping back and starting to run.)

Dance

Gatekeeper: I think that we already have a product that does what you are selling. I don't think we need your product. (Stepping back.)

Salesperson: Great. Maybe you are right. Maybe our product isn't for you. We don't want you to do business with us unless it is good for you. That's why I wanted to talk to Mike. I wanted to find out his needs and the needs of your organization, and then let him know what we offer and see if there is a fit. If there is a fit, great. If not, no big deal. (Mirrors the emotion the gatekeeper shows of "we don't need you." Notice that the salesperson doesn't "need" the sale either. This is mirrored emotion while stepping back.)

Gatekeeper: I might be able to squeeze you in week after next. (Stepping in.)

Salesperson: Great. What time works best for Mike? (Mirrors the emotion and steps in, too.)

Chase

Gatekeeper: He is not going to be able to meet with you for a few weeks. We have quarterly numbers to do plus prepare for an annual conference. (Stepping back.)

Salesperson: Well, I am only going to be in your area on those days. Is there any way to squeeze me in? Plus, if he likes our product he will need to take advantage of it very soon or he will miss out on our current promotion. (Steps in and pushes.)

Gatekeeper: Sorry, it isn't going to work this month. (Stepping back and holding onto her position.)

Dance

Gatekeeper: He is not going to be able to meet with you for a few weeks. We have quarterly numbers to do plus prepare for an annual conference. (Stepping back.)

Salesperson: Perfect. That is fine. I am very busy myself. Whether it is now or next month, no big deal. Take your time. (Mirrors the emotion and steps back, too.)

Gatekeeper: Great. I will set it up for the first week of next month. However, if things change, it might work for me to get you in a bit earlier. I will let you know. (Stepping in.)

Salesperson: Perfect. If he can meet earlier, I will try to accommodate his schedule. (Mirrors the emotion and steps in, too.)

Chase

Prospect: I'm not sure this is the right time for us. I need to talk this over with my partner. (Stepping back.)

Salesperson: If you don't act right now you'll miss out on an amazing deal. I'll even throw in a discount. (Steps in and pushes.)

Prospect: I really don't know if this is a good fit for us and want to talk to him first. (Stepping back further.)

Salesperson: You'd be foolish to pass this up. I'll tell you what I'll do... (Pushing even more.)

Prospect: No thank you. (Runs.)

Dance

Prospect: I'm not sure this is the right time for us. I need to talk this over with my partner. (Stepping back.)

Salesperson: That's a good idea. In fact, I wouldn't want you to move forward unless both of you are on board. Take all the time you need. (Mirrors the emotion and steps back, too.)

Prospect: My partner will be in later this afternoon. If he has questions can I have him call you? (Stepping in.)

Salesperson: Absolutely. Have him call me and I will try to accommodate his schedule. (Mirrors the emotion and steps in.)

How would you treat your mother or friend who was feeling apprehensive about something?

Remember, the best salespeople are the best salespeople because they act *nothing* like a stereotypical salesperson. They act like a real, honest human—like a friend—who just wants to help. They are willing to admit that they may not have all the answers, their product may not be a fit, etc. They are willing to step back, remove the pressure and create space. They are conscious to reflect the tone and intensity level of the gatekeeper.

Be willing to dance and step away when you can sense that your prospect is stepping away. This will improve the chances that they will step in again. Of course, when they do step in by giving you an appointment, it is important that you are able to step in as well with a very compelling reason or story that will help advance the sale.

Chapter Six

The Art of Getting Your Way

How the Top Salespeople Differentiate Themselves in Negotiations

"Diplomacy is the art of letting others have your way."

—Daniele Vare

In almost everything we do we are negotiating. We negotiate when trying to get a date, discussing promotions, and planning events. We also negotiate to get an appointment with decision makers who are often heavily guarded and scheduled. We'll discuss some negotiation skills, and then I'll show you how you can use those skills to get appointments.

Principle: Listen more.
You have two ears and one mouth.

Let's begin by discussing a very basic and important principle of negotiation: find out where the other party stands *before* stating your position.

You may have heard that the "first person to name a number loses." I don't like this statement because it implies that someone has to lose, and I believe in "win-win" negotiating. However, I do believe that there is some merit in not being the first one to reveal your position in a negotiation.

Let me demonstrate this principle with a hypothetical story:

Let's say that I find a diamond in my backyard. "Wow!" I think to myself, "What a lucky day!" I decide to take it to the market to sell it so that I can cash in on my big find. Perhaps in the back of my mind I feel that if I can sell it for $10,000, I will be satisfied. Let's say that you are an experienced diamond trader who happens to be in the marketplace at the same time. When you see the diamond, you know immediately that the diamond is worth $100,000.

Here is a quick review of the situation so far:

What I want for the diamond: $10,000

What you believe the diamond is worth: $100,000

Difference between the two: $90,000

Perhaps I start off the negotiation by trying to "high ball" you with an offer to sell you the diamond for double what I really want: $20,000. By laying my position on the table first, what did I lose?

You may be willing to pay $70,000, $80,000, $95,000, or more if you know that you can turn around and sell it for $100,000 right away. Thus, presenting my offer and revealing my position first may have cost me as much as $50,000-$75,000 (the difference between my $20,000 "high ball" offer and what you may be willing to pay for it).

Let's reverse the scenario and say that you, the diamond trader, are the first one to name the price you will pay. "I will pay you $70,000," you say, quietly thinking about the substantial profit you believe you can make. Offering $30,000 less than you think it is worth may seem like a great way to start the negotiation. However, when you stated your position first, what did you lose? Remember, that I will be satisfied with $10,000, so even though you thought you were giving me a "low ball" offer, you really just shot yourself in the foot to the tune of $60,000.

Here comes the tricky part: How do you get the other guy to name the position first? This is a *very* important question, because you need to understand the needs and desires of the other side before you can negotiate effectively, including when getting appointments and making sales.

Principle: Aim to understand others first.

I will address this question, but first let's look at another scenario:

I had a friend ask me to help him negotiate the purchase of a car. I told him that I would help him, but I asked my friend to let the salesperson know that I was the final say on whether or not he was going to buy the car. This way the salesperson would not try to get me out of the way and would listen to me. My friend agreed to my terms.

We arrived at the dealership and asked to drive a shiny, blue Mustang. It was a good-looking car and drove beautifully. We made sure to mention how much we liked the car, as we wanted the salesman to know that we were serious. Being a salesperson myself, I could almost see the dollar signs in the eyes of this salesman. He thought that he was going to get an easy sale. However, we were about to crush those dreams.

After taking a test drive, I told the salesman that we would need to get a great price on the car. "What do you need?" he replied.

(This was his way of asking me to name my position first).

(What if I said to him, "I need $3,000 off of the price"? Why could that be compromising my negotiating position? The reason is because he may be willing to come down more than just $3,000. What if he is willing to discount $4,000 or $5,000 from the sticker price? If I only ask for $3,000, then I might be leaving money on the table.)

I stood my ground using a simple two-step process:

1. Compliment or otherwise praise. (You want them to feel good for asking the question).

2. Turn it around by asking a question.

This process works for two reasons: 1) people loved to be praised; and 2) the person asking the questions is the one in control.

When the salesman asked, "What do you need?" I responded warmly, and with a smile, "Great question. How low can you go?"

Notice that I didn't answer his question. Let's analyze my response:

1. "Great question." (Praising him for asking the question—remember people love to feel praised.)

2. "How low can you go?" (Maintaining control by asking another question. Notice that I didn't answer his question at all.)

The salesman replied, "I can't just go back to my boss and ask him how low he can go. I have to bring him something. What do you need?"

(Now realize that he *again* was asking me to name my position, which I didn't want to do. I wanted to understand his position first).

I replied, “Wow, you are a great negotiator. I still need you to go to your boss and let me know how low you can go. Will you do that?"

It was clear that he was used to getting a direct answer. He continued to try to get me to name a number and I continued, diplomatically and calmly, to not respond to his inquiries but instead asked him to name his position first. I think that this same type of interaction went on a few times before the salesperson finally went back to see how low the manager was willing to go.

The sticker price for the car was $24,600.

The salesman came back with an answer: "$21,600," he said.

Notice that the price came down $3,000 without me so much as naming a number.

I looked at my feet, rubbed my forehead, and nodded my head back and forth slowly. My body language was clearly showing that I wasn't thrilled with his initial offer.

I then uttered two words, "That's trouble," and stood there silently gazing at the floor and rubbing my head apprehensively.

"Maybe we can do $20,600," the car salesperson blurted out, seeing my apprehension at the number he had named.

The price had just dropped another $1,000. I still had not named a number and had simply shown some discomfort in my body language and then uttered two words (do the math, that's $500 per word).

Much of what we say we do not say with our words but with our body language and tone of voice.

After some discussion, we ended up deciding not to buy the car. As we walked towards the door, the salesman tried to stop us with a last minute plea, "Maybe we can do $19,600," the salesman exclaimed, clearly trying unsuccessfully not to sound desperate.

Notice that the price came down by $5,000 dollars *without me ever naming a number*. The salesman was the only person naming numbers, and that, frankly, was the way I liked it. If I had suggested a $2,000 discount or even a $4,000 discount, my friend may have left money on the table as the salesman was willing to discount $5,000.

Why would I have a whole chapter about negotiating when this book is about cold calling to get appointments? Because the entire cold calling process is a negotiation. You need to master negotiation skills if you want to be among the best. Often a gatekeeper will ask you to give up your position before you truly understand her, or more importantly, the company's position. You must be sharp to recognize when these seemingly benign questions are asked. For example, a gatekeeper could ask, "Can you tell me what this is regarding?" or "Can you tell me more about your product?" Those may seem like innocent questions, and they often are asked innocently. However, she is asking you to name your sales position first. That way maybe she can pass you off to someone else (a mid-level manager perhaps) and save herself and her boss the trouble of meeting with you. Again, she is asking you to name your position first, and you have to be good at politely reversing control of the conversation.

When I first started out, I would often answer these questions immediately. The gatekeeper, successfully outmaneuvering me by understanding my position first, would then reply, "Great. The person that handles that is Kristy. Let me transfer you to her." I would then get sent to a low- or mid-level person's voice mail.

Now, let me be clear that being directed to speak with a mid-level person in the company by a high-level gatekeeper is not a bad position to be in. It is not, however, as ideal as being able to speak to the high-level person first so that you can understand the company's needs and goals.

Another danger of naming your position first is that you could explain everything about your product and all of its great features only to be told that "another company is already providing that service for us" or “we don’t need your type of product” and not be given an appointment with the decision maker.

To clarify, the point is not that you are avoiding answering direct questions. That comes across as manipulative. The real point is that you don't want to open your mouth and compromise your position without first understanding the other party. Let's look at it another way with a few examples:

Example #1

Suppose a D.J. gets a call from Sally interested in hiring him to play the music at her party:

Sally: Do you play country music?

D.J. (Enthusiastically): You bet! I play music from every country artist you can think of!

Sally: I asked because I really hate country music. Thanks anyway.

Doh! The D.J. completely shot himself in the foot by assuming he knew what Sally wanted and by jumping to conclusions before understanding her needs. What he could have done was use the two step process to find out her position first. For example, when asked, "Do you play country music?" he could have said "Good question. Why do you ask?" That would have allowed her to open up about her disdain for country music, and he would then have been in a better position to correctly address her needs. Taking this one step further, after he realized she doesn't like country music, he could ask, "What kind of music would you like played?" This again gives him control of the conversation and allows him to uncover and address her needs.

Example #2

Imagine a commercial real estate agent approaches an organization about buying office space:

Gatekeeper: I know Jim (decision maker) was looking into getting some office space. What kind of office space do you specialize in?

Bad Salesperson: Class A. We can get you into the nicest, high-end space around town. It's our specialty!

Gatekeeper: Oh, we are a conservative company and like to get the most square footage for our money. We don't need the marble, just space for our cubicles. We try to steer away from Class A as it's too expensive and would rather focus on B or C. Perhaps we'll just use the agent that helped us before. He specialized more in what we are looking for. Thank you for your time.

See how the salesperson lost his chance because he named his position first? Let's look at an example of how he could have handled the situation better:

Gatekeeper: I know Jim (decision maker) was looking into getting some office space. What kind of office space do you specialize in?

Good Salesperson: Great question. Glad you asked. What kind do you need? (Notice that he did not give away his negotiating position; he wanted her to name their position first.)

Gatekeeper: I know we don't have very fancy office space. Jim seems to like to get the best deal. He isn't that concerned about fancy—more about getting the most square feet for the money.

Good Salesperson: Great. I will make a note of it for when I speak with Jim. I'd like to find out more about what his needs are to see if there is a good fit. I'm going to be in your area on Tuesday and Thursday. Is there a day that would work better for Jim to meet?

Gatekeeper: Jim is busy both of those days.

Good Salesperson: No problem. When would work best for Jim? (Notice he is asking assumptive questions, which we'll discuss later in this chapter. He is not asking *if* Jim will meet with him, he already *assumed* that he will. He is asking *when.)*

Gatekeeper: He may have some time next week after the conference. Until then he is slammed. Could you do next Friday?

Good Salesperson: What time next Friday? (Notice that he didn't immediately say yes.)

Gatekeeper: I have a slot at 4 pm.

Good Salesperson: I can make that work. I will put it on the calendar.

Gatekeeper: Great.

Good Salesperson: Thanks for your help. When I meet with Jim, I will mention how professional and helpful you have been.

Gatekeeper: (probably caught off guard): Thank you!

Good Salesperson: No. Thank you!

Now right after the conversation, the salesperson *immediately* sends the email and puts a thank you card in the mail thanking the gatekeeper for the appointment. A real card. He can send a thank you email as well but a card shows that he is willing to go the extra mile and, trust me, the gatekeeper will remember this salesperson. He is different than the rest. He has offered to put in a good word to her boss and help her with something that is important to her—her career!

Notice how in this example we used negotiation principles by not naming our position first, and we used positive reinforcement by appreciating the gatekeeper for moving us in the direction of a sale (i.e. getting us an appointment). We also used assumptive questioning (instead of asking "Can I get an appointment with Jim?" we asked, "I will be in your area on Tuesday and Thursday, is there a day that would work better for Jim?")

This conversation may only take one minute but we are using multiple tools to get the appointment.

Returning to the gatekeeper's question, here is an effective response:

Gatekeeper: Can you tell me more about your product?

You: Great Question. I'm glad you asked. It would probably take quite a while to go over everything, which is why I am trying to set up an appointment with Chelsea. I am going to be in your area on May 2nd and 3rd and had a little time in the afternoon. Do you think that she would have some time to meet on one of those days?

Notice how you:

1. made the gatekeeper feel good for asking by saying, "Great question. I am glad you asked." and then
2. turned it around by asking a question?

If done with the right approach, tone, and with sincerity, the gatekeeper may forget that her question was never answered. The key is to compliment her for her curiosity and then turn the conversation to you so that you are asking the questions and in control.

It is critical that you develop a sincere way to make the gatekeeper feel good for asking the question. In my various trainings, some have expressed that this does not come naturally. If this is the case for you, you can practice until it feels natural for you or choose a different but similar response that fits you better. The choice of words or the phrase is not as important as *how* you say it. If it doesn't already, complimenting people should come sincerely and naturally and not just because it will help you in your negotiations.

Practice different questions that you feel comfortable with (or could at least eventually become comfortable with) that will help you maintain control. Also, remember that this is a technique that has worked for me that may or may not work for you. Remember, principles trump techniques. The key principle is that you should listen first and try to understand where others come from. The technique you use is of lesser importance.

Assumptive Questions

During any negotiation, the way you ask questions is crucial and can mean the difference between getting the appointment/sale or not. It is imperative to speak confidently when asking for the appointment.

What are the best kinds of questions to ask when trying to secure an appointment? Good question!

Have you ever noticed that timid questions are often asked in a yes/no format?

Have you also noticed that confident salespeople often phrase their questions confidently and assumptively as if the person has already said yes.

Assumptive questions are just that—assumptive. You don't ask *if* you can meet with her, you ask *when*.

When it comes time to ask for the appointment, a confident and successful salesperson does not say, "So, can I get an appointment with Mark?" Notice that this is a yes/no question and easily opens up the door for the reply to be no. If you have done all the ground work, you have a right to ask the question assumptively.

Caution! If you do not use assumptive questions sparingly and with good judgment, you risk becoming a pushy salesperson. Also, you should note that when you employ the principles in this book, often times you don't even need to ask for the appointment. They ask you!

Non-assumptive: Can I get an appointment with Sharon?

Assumptive: I'm going to be in your area next week. I have some time on Tuesday and Thursday. I know Sharon is very busy, and I want to accommodate her schedule, but does one of those days work?

Notice that you are letting them choose between two dates, not between yes and no. Your questions already assume she has said yes and you are giving her options to choose from.

Examples of how less confident, yes/no questions can be turned into powerful, assumptive questions:

Yes/No Question: Can I get an appointment?

Powerful, Assumptive Question: Does this week or next week work better for Tim?

Powerful, Assumptive Question: What time works best so I can accommodate her schedule?

Yes/No Question: Do you want to buy my product?

Powerful, Assumptive Question: When is the best time to get started on this?

You have to be careful. If you use assumptive questions incorrectly, you can come across as the pushy, manipulative salesperson I am trying to steer you away from. Use these questions sparingly and with good judgment, acting like a real person. "Thanks for helping me out. What works best for him so I can accommodate his schedule?"

Chapter Seven

Putting It All Together

We've discussed at length many different principles and techniques you can apply to secure the end result: getting the treasured appointment. But while I've broken down each element separately in the book, the application is not so clean-cut. You are not moving from one stair step to the next, taking one at a time until you reach the top. You do not move from the negotiating phase to the dancing phase and then start to take notes if you hear something out of the ordinary. Often, many things are happening at once, and a successful salesperson may use all the available tools at nearly the same time.

A child fills in a paint-by-number picture one color at a time. An artist, however, doesn't paint all the blue elements first and then move on to red. He begins with a central tree, interspersing varying shades of green and brown, moves to the mountains in the background, and then later returns to add birds to the tree. He uses a full palate of color while keeping the big picture in mind until he completes a beautiful work of art.

Similarly, when you are on the phone, everything is happening at once, and you may use one or two techniques or you may have to recall and apply many things simultaneously. You might use everything we've discussed in a 30-second conversation: you're psychologically dancing, stepping in-and-out to mirror the intensity, taking good notes and creating a map of the organization, negotiating, asking assumptive questions, sincerely complimenting, all while being aware of your tone of voice and the impression you are leaving in one short call.

This may seem overwhelming at first, but with practice it will come naturally.

Please note that every conversation will be different. That is why you must understand the principles and techniques we've discussed and know when and how to apply them. However, below are two different samples of how a conversation might play out.

Notice how each of the elements has a role:

SAMPLE INITIAL CONVERSATION #1:

Jan: Hello, this is Jan with XYZ. How may I help you?

Salesperson: Hi. I'm calling about possibly doing a sales training for your company. Who is the best person for me to talk to?

Jan: It might be Marla. Or maybe Mike. Let me transfer you to him. I think he handles that.

Salesperson: Thank you. What do Marla and Mike do? (Starting to make a map.)

Jan: Marla is in sales, and Mike is head of purchasing. (Noting it.)

Salesperson: Great. Can you tell me their last names and direct lines? Also, who is Mike's assistant?

Jan: It's Mike Smith and Marla Williams. Mike's assistant is Kay. Let me transfer you.

Salesperson: Great. Thanks, Jan.

(During the transfer, he is noting the names and positions of Jan, Mike, Kay, and Marla as well as that Kay is Mike's assistant.)

Kay: Good Afternoon. This is Kay.

Salesperson: Hi, Kay. I spoke briefly with Jan, and she mentioned that maybe I should talk to Marla but that perhaps Mike was the best person to help me. Is he available? (Intentionally using first names to build rapport.)

Kay: He is out for the afternoon. May I ask what this is regarding? (Careful. She is asking him to name his position first.)

Salesperson: (Chuckling in a friendly way.) Great question. I'm glad you asked. We help companies improve their bottom-line sales numbers. It could probably take quite a while to go over everything, which is one reason I am trying to set up an appointment with Mike. I am going to be in your area on May 2nd and 3rd and had some time in the afternoon on those days. Do you think that he would have some time to meet with me on one of those days? (Not giving away his negotiating position by using the two-step process while still giving a bit of information.)

Kay: Well, I think that we would need to know a bit more about your product. (Stepping back.)

Salesperson: I agree. Tell you what. Let me send a quick email to him introducing myself and telling him a bit about what we do. Is that OK? (Stepping back with her as well as mirroring her.)

Kay: Sure, that would be fine. His email address is _____ .

Salesperson: (Repeating it back to make sure he got it right.) Is that right?

Kay: You got it.

Salesperson: Oh, and do you mind if I copy you on it? Just to make sure he gets it?

Kay: That's fine.

Salesperson: What's the best email address for you?

Kay: My email is ____________.

Salesperson: (Repeating back the email.) Is that right?

Kay: That's it.

Salesperson: Great. I'll send that email right now. By the way, you have been very helpful and professional. Really, I speak to a lot of people every day and I really appreciate your courteous manner. I will make sure to mention that to Mike in the email. (Sincerely complimenting.)

Kay: Really? Thank you.

Salesperson: Of course. I'll send it over right now, and if you could make sure he gets it, that would be great. And then if you could, give me a call or email me a time when he can meet. I'm sure that he is very busy. You can let him know that I will try to be flexible with his schedule.

Kay: I will. Thanks.

Salesperson: (Pausing slightly as he finishes typing.) I just sent the email. Did you get it? (Sending email with a compliment to her on the first line.)

Kay: Let me check. Yes I got it. Thank you again for the compliment.

Salesperson: Great. Maybe I can check back in a few days and find a good time when we could meet.

Kay: Sounds good. I will print this out and leave it on his desk for him.

Salesperson: Thank you.

(After the conversation is over, a thank you card is sent immediately to Kay thanking her for her time. Remember the principle of recognizing people and reinforcing behavior.)

SAMPLE INITIAL CONVERSATION #2:

(This conversation assumes that an email has already been sent to the decision maker and this is a follow-up call a few days later):

Chelsea: Hello, this is Chelsea. How may I help you?

Salesperson: Is Gordon in? (Casually.)

Chelsea: Gordon is not in right now. May I ask who is calling?

Salesperson: This is Bill with Gicklegak, Inc. I believe that Gordon is the one who handles purchasing, correct?

Chelsea: Well, both Bill and Sofia in marketing do. (Note this for your map.)

Salesperson: Well, I sent an email to Gordon a few days ago, and I am following up with him on that. (Using first name to build rapport.)

Chelsea: What was the email regarding?

Salesperson: I'm glad you asked. It's a great question. I don't know if I could tell you all about our company and still be respectful of your time, which is why I was trying to speak briefly with Gordon. I am going to be in your area on Monday and Wednesday and wondered if he would be available to meet briefly on one of those days. (Notice assumptive questioning.)

Chelsea: Gordon in unavailable right now. He is on vacation with his family in Hawaii and won't be back until next Thursday. (Remember to note this detail to build rapport later on.)

Salesperson: Hmm. And you are stuck there in the office? (Chuckling and friendly) (Notice informal conversation, not formal. Talking just like you would talk to a good friend: comfortable and friendly but not overly so. Remember, intonation and the *way* that you say things can say more than your words.)

Chelsea: I'm totally jealous. I've never been.

Salesperson: My wife would be jealous too. Oh well. Good thing we get to enjoy the snow! (Chuckling.) Hey, maybe what I can do is resend the email to him. Would that be alright? (Again notice the informal conversation.)

Chelsea: OK.

Salesperson: The email address I have for him is ______. Is that the best one?

Chelsea: Actually, no. Let me give you a better address. The email address you have is just one we use for our website, it is not his personal address. Send it to ______.

Salesperson: Thanks. Oh, and do you mind if I copy you on it? Just to make sure he gets it?

Chelsea: That's fine.

Salesperson: What's the best email address for you?

Chelsea: My email is ____________.

Salesperson: (Repeating back the email.) Is that right?

Chelsea: You got it.

Salesperson: Great. I'll send that email right now. By the way, you have been very helpful and courteous. I speak to a lot of people and I really appreciate your professionalism. I will make sure to mention that to Gordon in the email. (Again, the way something is said is more important than what is said. It must be sincere.)

Chelsea: That's very nice of you. Thank you.

Salesperson: Of course. I'll send it over right now, and if you could make sure he gets it, that would be great. And then if you could, give me a call or email me a time when he can meet. I'm sure that he is very busy. You can let him know that I will try to be flexible with his schedule.

Chelsea: I will. Thanks.

Salesperson: (Pausing slightly as he finishes typing and sending email with a sincere compliment about Chelsea.) I **just resent the email. Did you get it?**

Chelsea: Let me check . . . Yes, I got it. Thank you again for your kind words.

Salesperson: (Sincerely.) Well, I really appreciated how professional you have been.

Chelsea: I will make sure he gets this.

Salesperson: Thank you. I look forward to hearing back from you. Could you just shoot me a quick email if there is a time that works for him?

Chelsea: Sure.

Salesperson: Great. Thanks. Try not to think about Hawaii too much and I won't tell my wife where Gordon is since she is driving around in this snow right now. (With a bit of humor, notice the casual friendly way of speaking.)

(After the conversation is over, a thank you card is sent immediately to Chelsea thanking her for her time.)

Notice that in both brief conversations the salesperson started to create a map of the organization (of course, taking good notes along the way of everything that was said), negotiated his way to controlling the conversation, used first names to build rapport, complimented the gatekeeper, copied the gatekeeper on an email with the compliment about her to her boss, asked an assumptive question to get on the decision maker's schedule, and was friendly and casual throughout the phone call.

The call was short and direct, but the salesperson accomplished a lot of things, including building a relationship and distinguishing himself, leaving a positive impression on the gatekeeper. The salesperson should follow up a week or so later, after the gatekeeper received his email and thank you card, and she would remember him, unlike the dozens of other salespeople she talked to that week.

The concepts I've shared are simple but they can make a world of difference. It all comes down to treating people with genuine respect and like worthwhile human beings. Approach them as you would a friend, and they should respond to you in kind. Throughout it all, always keep in mind that positively differentiating yourself to someone close to the decision maker (or to the actual decision maker) is the key that will unlock the gate.

The Next Step

You've arrived. You are now in an appointment with the key decision maker, finding out what her needs are, and presenting how you can help her. This is a great place to be. But you need to remember one thing: you haven't arrived at all. You are just starting to sell. At some point in the appointment, you should ask her who else needs to be involved if their company is to move forward with your product or service. She may mention that a committee would need to meet with you or that she needs to have another meeting with others present. Pay particular attention here, and write down notes about each person. In a large organization, your first presentation to at least one decision maker is crucial. But if done correctly, it likely will lead to another presentation or presentations with other decision makers. This is great news. Your journey toward selling this organization is now officially underway.

Good luck on your journey to a very lucrative sales career! And may you make more appointments and presentations than you ever thought possible.

Epilogue

Being Comfortable with Discomfort

"A coward is incapable of exhibiting love; it is the prerogative of the brave."

—Mahatma Gandhi

"We could never learn to be brave and patient if there were only joy in the world."

—Helen Keller

The concepts discussed in this book won't make a bit of difference if you do not employ the timeless principles of work and bravery.

Bravery is painful.

To be truly brave you must be willing to endure high levels of discomfort. This discomfort may be physical, mental, spiritual, or emotional. The purpose of this book is *not* to make you feel good. On the contrary, the purpose of this book is to help you become better at tolerating discomfort and pain. I want to inspire you to voluntarily and strategically take on new tasks that will require, at least initially, that you endure mental pain and discomfort.

I want you to get good at experiencing and marching straight into the face of pain and discomfort—not because I am a sadist or a masochist. In reality, it is because I want you to experience the feeling of overcoming and growing. Avoiding the pain of fear is really impossible. If you don't step into the fear and overcome it, you will have the opportunity to live a long time, perhaps your whole life, with latent fear. Latent fear saps your strength and muzzles who you are, and *over time it is far more painful than just bravely stepping into your fear and dealing with it*. Let me say that again: Dealing with the pain *now*, even if it is intense, is over time less painful than trying to avoid the pain.

In my career, I have had the opportunity to knock on a lot of doors. Most people, especially those starting out in sales and even a great number of seasoned sales people, find door-to door sales uncomfortable and distasteful.

When I was first involved in sales, I started as a door-to-door salesperson. The extent of my training consisted of my manager asking me to go see how another successful salesperson sold so that I could learn from him. I followed this salesperson for several doors. He (and I as his follower) got in the fifth door or so and sold.

That was it—training completed.

Afterwards, I was told to "Go try it on your own—that is the best way to learn." To say I was nervous would be a big understatement. I had probably a half hour or so of training, and now it was time for me to strike out on my own. I walked timidly across the street and knocked on a door.

Now, there is a moment, right before you do something that you've never done before that can be terrifying—this moment is key. It's the moment where you are actually growing, if you let yourself, by pressing forward through the fear. Conversely, if you give into your fear and run away or otherwise try to avoid taking it head on, it is the moment that you are actually shrinking or building a prison wall around your soul.

Success [Comfort Zone] Goals and Dreams

[Success Comfort Zone Goals and Dreams]

Expanding your comfort zone may be very uncomfortable at first. Be strong enough to start and endure until what is uncomfortable becomes comfortable.

That is why this moment is key. You have to have the determination to endure this moment. You have to be able to endure pain and discomfort.

The door opened and a very nervous me tried to sell something that I only had minimal training for. I felt the fear. I knew that I might "flub it up" and, true to my belief, I was flubbing it up. I can't remember many details about knocking on that door, but I do remember how I felt and that the person was not interested. I remember the feeling of fear and nervousness and that I "flubbed it up." Something, be it pride or something else, continued to drive me, and I continued to knock on doors that day. And I continued to fail. I began to wonder if sales were not for me. Maybe the salesperson that I had been assigned to follow had the gift of the silver tongue and I did not. Perhaps his gift destined him to sales success while my lack of sales skills would doom me to a low-paying hourly job, I thought. My fear of failure continued past that moment and seemed to deepen as I continued knocking doors with no success.

However, something else was happening that I didn't even notice at the time. Each door was getting a bit easier—not very much at all, but just a little.

Let me emphasize that *the discomfort and pain does not immediately go away.* It may be there for a short time or a long time. It is often still painful even after the initial moment, and you have got to have the endurance to stick with it past that initial moment. When you do, *gradually* the discomfort gives way, perhaps just a little, but if you persist, the pain will be replaced by confidence and a feeling of strength.

I continued to knock on doors and continued to flub it up, and then something happened: I sold.

I am glad that I had the strength to keep knocking on doors even after I flubbed it up so many times after the initial door. What happened later was a long-term successful career in sales. I went from selling door-to-door to eventually selling real estate and even eventually to large and complex organizations.

I now feel *absolutely no discomfort* when making a cold call or knocking on a door. It is second nature, and I actually enjoy it. More accurately, I have almost conditioned myself to feel discomfort when I *don't* prospect. My comfort zone has expanded.

This feeling of strength does not come by reading this book. It does not come by imagining that you are brave (although imagining you are brave and visualizing success is a good thing). *This strength only comes to those who, in real life, endure pain and discomfort until they give way to confidence and strength.* This confidence and strength then begin to spill over into other areas of life not even related to the initial moment of discomfort. For example, a single man who pushes himself past the initial pain and discomfort of door-to-door selling may realize that he is more confident in approaching women to ask out on a date. He may find that he is a more confident in speaking publicly in front of a group. The benefits of pushing past your fear can be exponential.

When making your first cold call, including to a high-level contact, you may and most likely will experience some discomfort. This is good news. It means that you are growing. You may and probably will get rejected—many times. This is also good news. You need to force yourself to continue despite the discomfort. The discomfort is a sign that you are stretching, that you are growing. Discomfort and pain are your friends when learning something new.

The rewards of learning to be a great appointment setter and salesperson far outweigh the small amount of false safety that you will feel by not stepping into your fear and conquering it.

The Bad News: Learning new things outside your comfort zone is uncomfortable and sometimes even painful. The Good News: If you persist, the pain and discomfort go away, and when they do, you now live in a bigger-than-before comfort zone, and you have grown personally into a stronger, more experienced, and more capable human being.

Be brave, build your sales empire on correct principles, and find personal success.

Notes

1. Kunz, P. R., & Woolcott, M. (1976). Season's greetings: From my status to yours. Social Science Research, 5,269-278. http://dx.doi.org/10.1016/0049-089X(76)90003-X

2. Perlberg, William (Producer), & Seaton, George (Director). (May 2, 1947). Miracle on 34th Street. United States: Twentieth Century Fox.

About the Author

EksAyn has been "in the trenches" of sales for well over a decade. He has successfully sold in venues ranging from door-to-door sales to large and complex organizations including associations and governments. Both his formal education in psychology and his life experience have taught him how to understand, communicate, and connect with people. He conducts highly-rated trainings on sales and negotiation principles and techniques and is a member of the National Speakers Association.

For more information please visit his website at

www.eksayn.com

www.ingramcontent.com/pod-product-compliance
Lightning Source LLC
Chambersburg PA
CBHW071603200326
41519CB00021BB/6847

* 9 7 8 0 9 9 0 3 9 5 2 0 1 *